SAMUEL MORSE

by Mona Kerby

ASTHMA

COCKROACHES

FRIENDLY BEES, FEROCIOUS BEES

SAMUEL MORSE

by Mona Kerby

A FIRST BOOK
FRANKLIN WATTS
New York / London / Toronto / Sydney / 1991

Cover photograph courtesy of: New York Public Library,
Picture Collection
Photographs courtesy of: The Bettmann Archive: pp. 10, 22, 25,
32, 42; Historical Picture Service: pp. 12, 36, 40, 41, 43,
44, 45; New York Historical Society: pp. 15, 34; National Academy
of Design: p. 20; New York Public Library, Picture Collection:
pp. 24, 29, 35; New York University Archives, Bobst Library: p. 31;
A.T.&T Photo Archives: p. 39.

Library of Congress Cataloging-in-Publication Data

Kerby, Mona.
    Samuel Morse / by Mona Kerby.
        p.   cm. — (A First book)
    Includes bibliographical references (p.   ) and index.
    Summary: Describes Samuel Morse's career as a painter and
inventor, and how his development of the Morse's code laid the
    groundwork for modern telecommunications.
        ISBN 0-531-20023-X
    1. Morse, Samuel Finley Breese, 1791–1872—Juvenile literature.
    2. Inventors—United States—Biography—Juvenile literature.
    [1. Morse, Samuel Finley Breese, 1791–1872. 2. Inventors.]
            I. Title. II. Series.
        TK5243.M7K47 1991
        621.383′092—dc20
            [B]
            [92]

            90-13109   CIP   AC

CONTENTS

For Aurelia and Kerby with love

AUTHOR'S NOTE

When Samuel Morse was a little boy, he was called Finley by his family and friends. However, in this book, he will be called Samuel, since that is how the world knows him.

Throughout his life, Samuel Morse kept a journal and wrote many letters. After Morse died, his son Edward gathered his father's writings and published them in two volumes. To write this story, I read these books as well as a biography by Carleton Mabee called *The American Leonardo*. The words that are in quotation marks come directly from these sources.

And special thanks go to my students at J. B. Little Elementary School in Arlington, Texas, for enthusiastically learning and experimenting with the Morse code.

Sending smoke signals.

INTRODUCTION

On a chilly spring night some four thousand years ago, a Greek king sent a message to his wife. When we win the war with the Trojans, King Agamemnon had told his wife, Clytemnestra, I'll let you know. Of course, he didn't pick up the telephone. It had not yet been invented. His wife didn't know when the message would arrive. So every night for several years, a watchman sat on top of the palace roof.

Back then, the fastest way to communicate over miles of mountains and seas was by fire. From mountaintop to mountaintop, one man set a fire large enough for the next man to see.

Ever since time began, people have wanted to send messages quickly. They've used smoke signals, fast runners, flags, mirrors, and the ringing of bells. Some people learned to whistle or yell a message that could be heard for miles.

African tribes sent messages by pounding the earth with a huge stick. (Put your ear to the ground while a friend beats the earth a short distance away.) When the telescope was invented, messengers spelled out words on huge boards for the next person to read. In 1792, a Frenchman named Claude Chappe invented the semaphore telegraph. On platforms placed 15 miles (24 km) apart, men signaled with wooden codes, sending a message 150 miles (240 km) in fifteen minutes.

But in the 1830s, a man named Samuel Morse changed all this. In fact, his invention changed the history of the world. To send a message, Morse didn't need weeks, days, hours, or minutes. With the Morse code and a telegraph, a message arrived in seconds.

In this book, you will learn the story of Samuel Morse and the invention of the telegraph. You will learn how to make a simple telegraph set. You will learn about an invention that King Agamemnon could have used on that very long night thousands of years ago.

*Morse and his invention changed
the course of history.*

1

THE BOY

His parents called him Finley. Named for his mother's side of the family, Samuel Finley Breese Morse was born on April 27, 1791, in Charlestown, Massachusetts. This baby has more names than a Spanish ambassador, teased one family friend.

Of eleven children born to the Morses, three boys lived—Samuel and his younger brothers, Sidney and Richard. It never mattered how many times Samuel made mischief. To his mother, he was always one of the "dear boys."

But that's not to say that his parents let Samuel do what he pleased. They had high hopes for their firstborn son. Jedidiah Morse, Samuel's father, was a minister as well as the author of the first American geography book. He was a friend of George Washington. Elizabeth Morse's grandfather was a president of Princeton College.

Samuel's parents were proud Americans. After all, they

14

*Samuel Morse (far right) as a young boy
with his brothers Richard (right) and
Sidney (left) and their parents.*

had lived through exciting times. Sixteen years earlier, in the very month that Samuel was born, Americans were warned that the British were coming during the Revolutionary War. On the night of the ride of Paul Revere, Americans watched the steeple of Boston's Old North Church. Two lanterns meant the British were coming to Boston by sea. One lantern meant they were coming by land.

That simple signal—"One, if by land, and two, if by sea"—became one of the most famous messages in American history. No one knew it then, of course, but Samuel was to grow up and create a code that would be heard throughout the entire world.

Still, for the time at least, Jedidiah and Elizabeth had their hands full with Samuel. When he was four, they sent him to Old Ma'am Rand's school. One day, Samuel took a pin and etched his teacher's face on a chest of drawers.

In 1798, Samuel was sent away to school at Phillips Academy. In class, Samuel was sometimes the best student. Other times, he was the worst student. His mother promised him "Books, cakes & Pyes" that would "eat very good" if he would study. His father wrote letters asking him to do one thing at a time and "do it in the best manner."

And what did seven-year-old Samuel have to say for himself? In a letter home, he wrote, "I have as many blackberries as I want I go and pick them myself."

When Samuel entered Yale College in 1805, his teachers said that the fourteen-year-old disliked studying. Certainly, he was too busy for school. He liked to go "gunning" (shooting) and skating. In one letter home, Samuel wrote that he and his "chums" wanted to have "brandy, wine and segars." What's more, Samuel wrote, he needed a larger allowance.

Mr. and Mrs. Morse worried about their son. "Use good sense," his father pleaded.

Samuel responded to his parents' love and concern. "I shall not go out to gun anymore, for I know it makes you anxious about me." He also tried to pick friends who would please his parents.

School wasn't completely boring. Mr. Day's lectures on electricity fascinated Samuel. But what really interested the boy was drawing. He wanted to be an artist. He earned pocket money by drawing sketches or portraits of his friends as well as people in the town. In a letter dated July 22, 1810, Samuel wrote that he "was made for a painter" and asked his parents to let him study with an artist.

Mr. and Mrs. Morse had other plans. They were afraid Samuel could not make a living as a painter. They wanted him to be a bookseller. Samuel understood. "I am pleased," he wrote his mother. Still, the last line of his letter read, "I am so low in spirits that I could almost cry."

Samuel came home to Charlestown. He did not complain. During the day, he worked for a bookseller. But at night, in his room above the kitchen, Samuel painted. When his parents saw how much art meant to him, they decided to help their "dear boy."

In those days, great artists studied in Europe. Samuel wanted to study in London, England, which was thousands of miles across the Atlantic Ocean. Somehow, Mr. and Mrs. Morse found the money for their son to go to London.

On July 15, 1811, Samuel set sail from New York. The

journey lasted twenty-two days. For a trip on a sailing ship, this was a fast one. As soon as Samuel arrived in London, he wrote home. He knew his mother would be worried about him. "I wish that in an instant I could communicate the information," Samuel wrote, "but three thousand miles are not passed over in an instant and we must wait four long weeks before we can hear from each other."

Years later, Morse scribbled on the back of that letter's envelope, "A longing for the telegraph even in this letter."

2
THE PAINTER

One day in London, Samuel showed his drawing to his teacher. His teacher liked it. "Very well, sir, very well; go and finish it."

"It is finished," said Samuel.

"Oh, no," the teacher said. "Look here, and here and here."

So Samuel worked for another week. Again his teacher told him to finish. Samuel obeyed. But when his teacher told him to finish for the third time, Samuel was upset. "I cannot finish it," he declared.

Finally, the teacher explained. One drawing that was well done was better than dozens of half-finished paintings. Samuel loved being an artist. Soon his work was good enough for him to enter the Royal Academy school. His clay model of Hercules won a medal. In 1813, he finished a

A self-portrait of Morse. Long before
he invented the telegraph,
Morse was a well-known painter.

painting called *The Dying Hercules*. In 1815, he finished *The Judgement of Jupiter*.

Samuel enjoyed everything about London. He liked meeting famous authors and painters. In his letters home, Samuel made the capital city of England seem exciting. He told of a ghost that was supposedly haunting the houses. In another letter, he told about some murders in London. "I shall sleep with pistols at the head of my bed," Samuel wrote.

In 1815, at the end of three years, Samuel asked his parents if he could stay another year. He really needed to study in Paris, he wrote. Since he was going to be one of the greatest painters in the world, he needed more practice in painting landscapes.

His parents replied that he'd better learn how to paint portraits. Americans would buy pictures of themselves, Mr. and Mrs. Morse explained; Americans would not buy pictures of the countryside.

Besides, his mother wrote, Samuel was spending too much money. Even though his parents agreed to let him stay, Samuel decided to come home.

In October 1815, Samuel arrived in Boston. No one wanted any huge paintings, so Samuel decided to paint portraits. No one wanted any of those, either. Since no one came to him, Samuel traveled from town to town. In each place, he found a few customers.

He also found his future wife. Lucretia Pickering Walker was wonderful, Samuel wrote in his letters home. They married in 1818. "She has grown quite fleshy and healthy," Samuel wrote, "and we are as happy in each other as you can possibly wish us." In the next few years, their children, Susan, Charles, and Finley, were born.

One of many paintings by Morse,
Niagara Falls from Table Rock

Samuel struggled to support his family. While Lucretia and the children stayed with his parents, Samuel traveled and painted portraits. The trips weren't always fun. Sometimes a customer was hard to please. Make the curtain purple. Put a gold chain on my neck. Change the color of the guitar. Samuel made the changes, but he didn't always get paid. Other times, the traveling was the hard part. In those days, people traveled by horse and coach. Once the coach was so cold and wet that when Samuel closed his eyes, his eyelashes froze to his cheeks.

Samuel tried other ways to make money. He invented a water pump for firemen to use at fires. He also invented a marble-cutting machine. Neither idea was successful. Samuel's heart belonged to painting.

Slowly but surely, Samuel began to make a name for himself. People said that he was one of America's finest painters. In 1819, he painted a portrait of President Monroe. In 1822, he painted *Congress Hall*, one huge portrait of all the members of the House of Representatives. In 1825, he was selected to paint the portrait of Lafayette, the French general.

Samuel was excited and pleased. At last, he would be able to give Lucretia what she wanted—a home of her own. Again, he left for Washington. "The only thing I fear is that it is going to deprive me of my dear Lucretia." Sad to say, these words turned out to be true.

On February 8, 1825, Lucretia died from heart trouble. For two days, Samuel didn't hear of his wife's death. By the time he arrived home, Lucretia was already buried.

Samuel was heartbroken.

Alone, he bought a house in New York. After Samuel

Left: Mrs. Samuel F. B. Morse and Her Two Children,
as painted by the inventor
Above: Among Morse's other inventions was a water pump.
Here firemen operate a hand pump.
(From a Currier and Ives print.)

and some other painters formed the National Academy, he served as the first president. From seven in the morning until midnight, Samuel worked, but he couldn't manage his money well. When his brother Sidney learned that Samuel owed $11,000.00, Sidney wrote, "I despair of ever seeing him rich or at ease." And then, Samuel decided to go to Europe.

He needed more training in art, he said. On the walls of the rotunda (a round room) in the U.S. Capitol, four murals were to be painted. Samuel wanted to be chosen as one of the artists.

He sold his house, his furniture, and the painting of *Congress Hall*. He left his sons with his brothers, and his daughter, Susan, with Lucretia's sister. In November 1829, thirty-eight-year-old Samuel left home once again.

He traveled and painted in Italy, Switzerland, France, and England. He talked politics with General Lafayette. Samuel was fascinated with the French semaphore telegraph system.

Tall platforms, or semaphores, were built 15 miles (24 km) apart. In each semaphore, a man climbed to the top and held up huge codes for the next man to see. Over and over again, the message was repeated. On foggy days, when visibility was poor, the system did not work. Samuel began to wonder: Could electricity be used in a telegraph system?

In October 1832, Samuel sailed home. One evening at dinner, the passengers talked about electricity. An electromagnet, which can be as simple as wire wound around a nail and attached to a battery, produces an electric current, or jolt. This electric current will pass through wire.

Suddenly, Samuel had an idea. Electricity could transmit messages. For the rest of the trip, Samuel worked on an electric telegraph system. He wanted to keep it simple. The sender would tap out a message in code. On the other end, the electric current would move a pencil which would print the code.

Samuel was excited. In November, when his brothers met him at the ship, Samuel eagerly explained his idea. This time, rather than worrying about Samuel, his brothers believed that he had discovered something important.

"Well, Captain," said Samuel as he left the ship, "should you hear of the telegraph one of these days, as the wonder of the world, remember the discovery was made on board the good ship *Sully*."

3
THE INVENTOR

In no time at all, Samuel made the first telegraph. He used ordinary materials—a picture frame, a table, and lead pieces, which he melted and molded (and spilled) in his sister-in-law's living room.

It worked. It was simple to make. But the world ignored Samuel's invention. For twelve long years, Samuel battled one disaster after another.

His biggest problem was money. He was broke. He couldn't buy food, much less buy materials to make telegraphs. Another problem was time. Samuel was too busy with his painting.

In 1835, he became a professor of painting and sculpture at the newly established University of the City of New York (now New York University). Because his salary was so small, he ate and slept in his classroom. Once, after one of

Morse's first telegraph receiver.
He made this device from a modified
canvas stretcher, which is used in painting.

his students had bought him supper, Samuel said, "This is my first meal in twenty-four hours." He also told his student not to be an artist. Even "a house dog lives better," he said.

Whenever Samuel felt discouraged, he wrote that he had the "blues," but he didn't give up. More than anything, he wanted to be chosen as one of the four artists to paint the huge murals in the rotunda of the U.S. Capitol. For some reason, however, former president John Quincy Adams and his committee chose artists who had less training than Samuel.

Samuel was crushed. Adams, Samuel wrote, "killed me as a painter, and he intended to do it." In fact, Samuel never seriously painted again. He wrote, "The very name of pictures produces a sadness of heart I cannot describe."

As a result of this, Samuel turned his attention to the telegraph. Perhaps, Samuel reasoned, God had chosen another "path" for him.

It wasn't an easy path. For one thing, Samuel had to make the most of his supplies. Today wire comes in huge rolls and is insulated (covered) with plastic. Back then, wire didn't come in rolls. Samuel bought it in pieces, joined it together, and insulated it with cotton.

In the fall of 1837, Samuel held his first demonstration, or show. He strung ten miles of wire around his classroom. He invited wealthy businessmen to come, hoping they would invest in the telegraph. They didn't loan Samuel a dime.

No one seemed very interested, except a young man named Alfred Vail. Vail's father owned an iron-and-brass works. Young Vail offered to help Morse. Leonard D. Gale also became a partner. The three partners occasionally asked the advice of scientist Joseph Henry.

PROFESSOR MORSE *requests the honour of*

Mr Samuel C Mott

company, in the Geological Cabinet of the University,
Washington Square, to witness the operation of
his **ELECTRO MAGNETIC TELEGRAPH,** *at a* **PRIVATE**
Exhibition of it, to a few friends, previous to its leaving
the City for Washington.

The apparatus will be prepared precisely
at **4** *o'clock, on* **Wed y** *the* **24** *inst.*

The time being limited, punctuality is specially
requested.

☞ Please show this note at the door of the room.

New-York City University, *Jan.* **24** 1838.

By permission of
Professor Morse
Your ob't Ser't
John Ely

*The inventor demonstrated his telegraph to many
people, hoping to interest some of them
in investing in his new discovery.*

Together, they began to improve the telegraph. The first telegraph used a marker to record the message. A later model used a notched metal rod to send the message. The men also made changes in the code. When they finished it, they had a series of dots and dashes that stood for every letter of the alphabet and every number from zero to nine. The most frequently used letters had the shortest codes. For example, the code for E was a dot ● . The code for T was a dash — . Letters that weren't used often had longer codes.

Over the next several years, Samuel asked the U.S. Congress for money to test the telegraph. Each time, Congress refused. Morse traveled to England and France, but no one was interested in his invention.

Morse continued giving painting lessons. He began practicing daguerreotypy, one of the earliest forms of photography. (Morse is considered the father of American photography.)

In October 1842, Morse ran a huge announcement in the New York newspapers, inviting people to see the amazing telegraph at work. By hand, Morse had wrapped 2 miles (3.2 km) of wire in cotton, tar, and rubber. On the evening before the show, Morse hired a man to row him across the New York harbor so that he could lay the cable, or wire. Two telegraph operators stood on opposite sides of the water. Morse hooked up everything and tested his equipment. It worked.

The next morning, fishermen pulled up the cable. Because they didn't know what it was, they cut it. As a result, the demonstration was canceled. People called Morse a liar and a fraud.

Left: Along with his other talents, Morse is known as the father of American photography. This photo of extremely rough quality is the very first daguerreotype ever made. Above: Artist, inventor, and leader of American photography in the early days of its development, Morse appears here in a silver print taken of him in 1872.

For years, Samuel deprived himself of "all pleasures and even necessary food." One thing kept him going: No matter what other people believed, Samuel knew that his invention would "contribute to the happiness of millions."

In December 1842, Morse again went to Washington, D.C., and asked Congress for money to test the telegraph. In March 1843, he was still calling on Congress, waiting for their answer. On the evening of March 3, 1844, the last day of Congress, Morse's request had not been presented. It looked hopeless. Morse left.

The next morning, a young friend came to Morse's room. "I have come to congratulate you," she said.

At midnight, his request had been voted on and passed by a margin of six votes. Morse was overjoyed. He promised the young woman that she could choose the first message to send over the wires.

Morse and his partners had two months to lay a telegraph line between Baltimore, Maryland, and Washington, D.C. Tension was high. Everything had to be made from scratch. The partners argued, and one partner, Fog Smith, tried to cheat the government. They had almost finished burying the cable beside the railroad track when they dis-

Morse heard from a friend that Congress had finally approved funds for him to build an experimental telegraph line. This young woman, Annie Ellsworth, later sent the first message on May 24, 1844.

covered that Smith hadn't properly insulated the wires. At the last minute, the wires were strung from tall poles above the ground.

On the morning of May 24, 1844, Morse sat in a room in the United States Supreme Court building. He tapped out the message the girl had picked, "What hath God wrought!" The message was received in Baltimore.

This was the turning point for the telegraph. At long last, the world believed in Samuel's invention. Within twelve years, telegraph lines crisscrossed the North American and European continents. By 1866, a telegraph cable had been laid across the Atlantic Ocean. Never again would it take months to send a message. The Morse code and the Morse telegraph were known throughout the world.

In his later years, Morse improved his invention and became active in the business aspects of the telegraph. There were a number of lawsuits. For the most part, however, these years were happy. In 1848, at the age of fifty-seven, Samuel married Sarah Griswold and together they had a large family. On June 10, 1871, a statue of Samuel Morse was dedicated in New York's Central Park to the eighty-year-old inventor. On April 2, 1872, Samuel Finley Breese Morse died.

As a young boy, Samuel couldn't seem to finish a task. As a man, he never quit trying. Poverty, hunger, and despair could not stop him from giving his telegraph to the world. Because of Samuel Morse's determination, the lives of millions of people were changed forever.

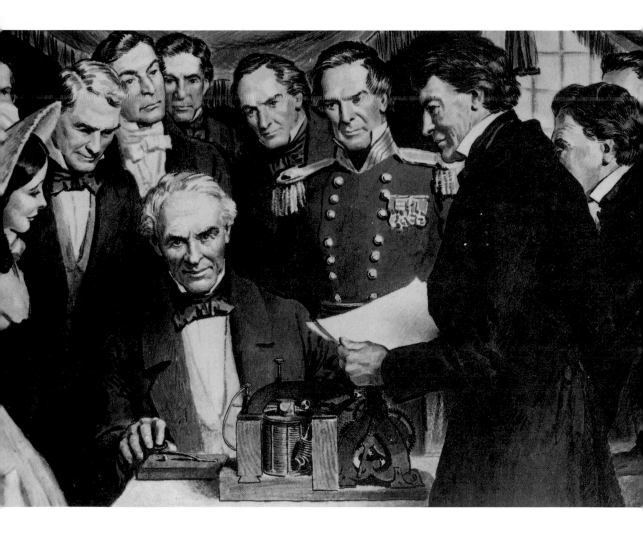

Sending the first practical telegraph. The message was sent over a 40-mile wire from Washington, D.C., to Baltimore, Maryland.

*Morse signing a greeting telegraphed
at the Morse celebration in 1871*

*The completion of the Atlantic telegraph
cable at Modern Wharf, East Greenwich,
Rhode Island in 1865*

*The arrival of the Atlantic cable
in Newfoundland, July 1866—
telegraph lines eventually crisscrossed
both America and Europe.*

*Laying the telegraph
across the plains of
the United States—a new era
of communication was born.*

A man of many talents, Samuel Morse made a unique contribution to the world of communications.

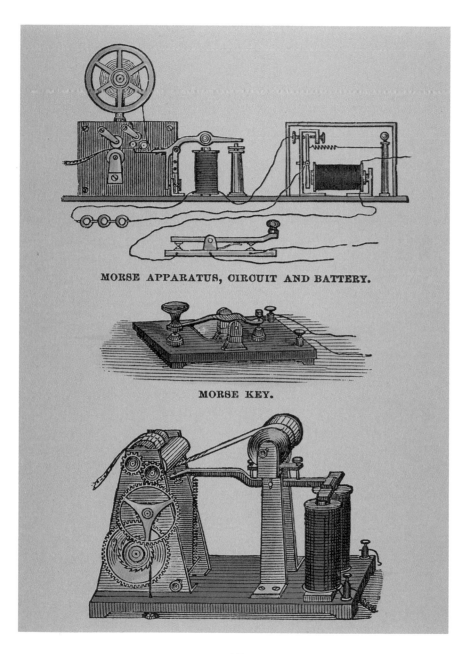

MORSE APPARATUS, CIRCUIT AND BATTERY.

MORSE KEY.

THE INTERNATIONAL MORSE CODE

Alphabet:

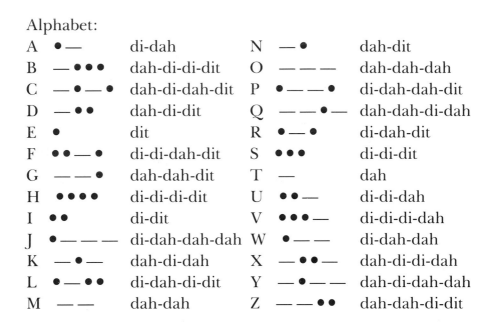

A	●—	di-dah	N	—●	dah-dit
B	—●●●	dah-di-di-dit	O	———	dah-dah-dah
C	—●—●	dah-di-dah-dit	P	●——●	di-dah-dah-dit
D	—●●	dah-di-dit	Q	——●—	dah-dah-di-dah
E	●	dit	R	●—●	di-dah-dit
F	●●—●	di-di-dah-dit	S	●●●	di-di-dit
G	——●	dah-dah-dit	T	—	dah
H	●●●●	di-di-di-dit	U	●●—	di-di-dah
I	●●	di-dit	V	●●●—	di-di-di-dah
J	●———	di-dah-dah-dah	W	●——	di-dah-dah
K	—●—	dah-di-dah	X	—●●—	dah-di-di-dah
L	●—●●	di-dah-di-dit	Y	—●——	dah-di-dah-dah
M	——	dah-dah	Z	——●●	dah-dah-di-dit

Numerals:

1	●————	di-dah-dah-dah-dah
2	●●———	di-di-dah-dah-dah
3	●●●——	di-di-di-dah-dah
4	●●●●—	di-di-di-di-dah
5	●●●●●	di-di-di-di-dit
6	—●●●●	dah-di-di-di-dit
7	——●●●	dah-dah-di-di-dit
8	———●●	dah-dah-dah-di-dit
9	————●	dah-dah-dah-dah-dit
0	—————	dah-dah-dah-dah-dah

4
EXPERIMENTING WITH MORSE CODE

For more than a hundred years, people have been using the Morse code to send messages. Since the 1930s, wireless radio stations have transmitted the code. Over radio, the code makes a beeping sound. But in the early days of telegraphs, when messages traveled by wires, telegraph operators heard a click-clack sound.

In this chapter, you will learn the Morse code and you will learn how to make a simple telegraph set. Your set will make those same clickety-clack sounds that Morse heard years ago.

MAKING A SIMPLE TELEGRAPH SET

Before you start, *ask an adult to help you make this project.* Cutting tin can be dangerous. The adult will also be able to help you find the items you need.

MATERIALS NEEDED:

2 pieces of soft wood

1 small drawer knob, or cut a wooden knob to fit the end of the key

1 aluminum nail, 3 in (7.62 cm)

4 screws, 5/8 in (1.59 cm)

1 stove bolt, 3 in (7.62 cm)

2 washers, 1/4 in (.635 cm)

1 nut, 1/4 in (.635 cm)

1 battery, number 6

insulated bell wire

2 strips of tin*

sandpaper

marker

scissors

pliers

screwdriver

hammer

* Small packages of tin can be purchased in the hobby department of a large craft store.

MAKING THE KEY:

1. Write "Key" on one piece of wood.
2. Cut a 1-in-wide (2.54-cm-wide) strip of tin.
3. On one end of the strip, screw on a small wooden knob. (If the tin is thick, you may first need to make a hole for the screw by hammering a nail into the tin.)
4. Attach the tin strip to the wood with a screw.
5. Using the pliers, bend the metal as shown.
6. Mount a screw in the wood under the raised end of the metal strip.
7. Adjust the metal strip. The key should touch the screw when pressed and spring up when released.

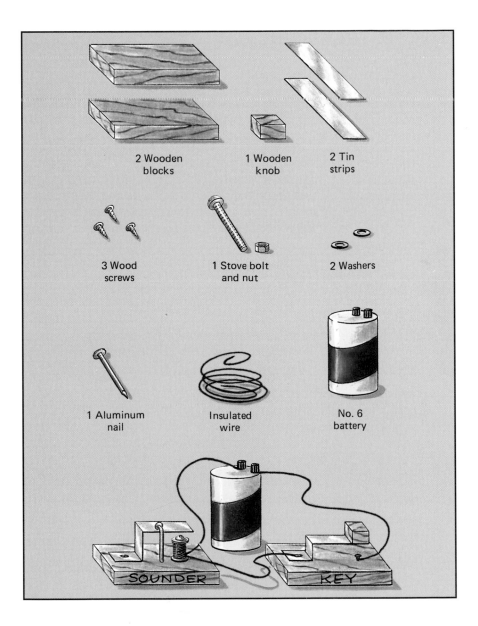

2 Wooden blocks

1 Wooden knob

2 Tin strips

3 Wood screws

1 Stove bolt and nut

2 Washers

1 Aluminum nail

Insulated wire

No. 6 battery

SOUNDER

KEY

MAKING THE ELECTROMAGNET:

1. Put the two washers on the stove bolt. Screw nut on end of bolt.
2. Between the two washers, wind four layers of bell wire. Make the wire tight and even. On first layer, start at the bottom and wind up. On second layer, start at the bottom and wind in opposite direction.
3. Repeat from top to bottom, always winding in opposite directions.
4. Twist the wires together.

MAKING THE SENDER:

1. Write "Sounder" on a piece of wood.
2. Cut a 1-in-wide (2.54-cm-wide) strip of tin.
3. Attach the tin to the wood with a screw.
4. With the pliers, bend the metal as shown.
5. Screw the electromagnet into the other end of the base. Secure, but do not overtighten.
6. Bend the head of the aluminum nail, then hammer it into the wood. The nail should be next to, but not touching, the tin strip.

ATTACHING THE WIRE:

1. Using the pliers, remove the insulation from all ends of the wire. If the plastic touches the connecting points, the telegraph key will not work.
2. Twist one end of the electromagnet wire to the post on the battery.
3. Twist the remaining electromagnet wire around the screw that is pressed into the end of the tin key.
4. Twist a third wire from the free battery terminal to the screw under the key knob.

TESTING:

1. Press the key. The electromagnet should pull down the metal sounder, making the clicking sound.
2. Release the key. The sounder should spring up, making another click when it hits the nail.
3. Readjust the metal strips.
4. When you are not using the telegraph, remove the wires from the battery so that the battery won't run down.

LEARNING THE MORSE CODE

You don't need a telegraph key to send the Morse code. You can write the code on paper. You can tap the code with your finger or a pencil. You can blink the code with your eyelids. You can flash the code with a flashlight. You can even talk in Morse code.

Perhaps the easiest way to learn the code is to say it out loud. You'll have more fun if you practice it with a friend. Don't memorize the code by the way it looks. Memorize it by the way it sounds.

There are several tricks to memorizing anything. Never practice longer than fifteen minutes at a time. It's better to practice for short periods over several days rather than for several hours on one day.

Look at the code. Do you see that it is entirely made up of dots and dashes? Each letter and number has its own combination of these symbols. When you say the Morse code, however, don't say "dot" and "dash." Instead, say "dit" for the dot and "dah" for the dash. The "t" of the "dit" is pronounced only when it ends a code.

Just like music, the Morse code has rhythm and beat. A "dit" receives one count and a "dah" receives three counts. (The word "dit" lasts the same length of the time it takes you to count to one. The word "dah" lasts as long as it takes you to count to three.) In code, the letter "A" sounds like "di-dah." Accent the "dah" sound.

The letter "V" is an easy code to remember. Think "V is for victory." Say the code "di-di-di-dah," or "this-is-a-vee." Do you hear the first four notes of Beethoven's Fifth Symphony?

The letter "F" is also a fun code. Say "di-di-dah-dit." This has the same rhythm as the words, "get a hair cut."

One way to memorize the code is to study the first four or five letters. After you learn them, move on to the next set of letters. Another way to memorize the code is to arrange the letters in memory groups, placing similar codes together.

MEMORY GROUPS

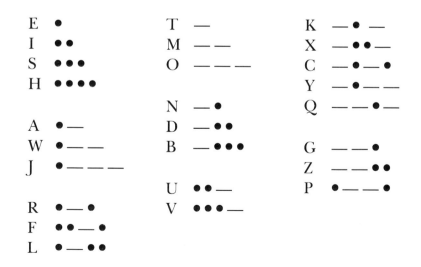

Once you have memorized the letters, you can begin to put words and sentences together. If you send the code too fast, your friend won't know when one letter stops and another begins. For this reason, count to three before you send the next letter. Count to six between words. When you write the code, leave three spaces between letters and six spaces between words.

MORSE CODE MESSAGES

The International Distress call (SOS) is used whenever there is trouble. Practice saying, "di-di-di-dah-dah-dah-di-di-dit." This is considered one code, so don't pause between letters.

Just for fun, try solving the following messages. Of course, you and your friend will want to make up your own messages to send.

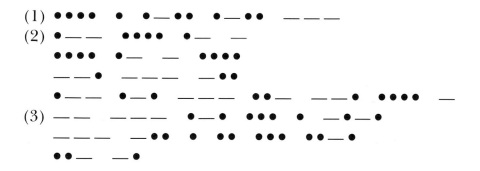

Answers: (1) Hello.
(2) What hath God wrought! (This was Morse's most famous message.)
(3) Morse code is fun.

CONCLUSION

Computers, satellites, and modern communication systems are slowly replacing the telegraph. Still, the Morse code is not forgotten. Amateur radio operators all over the world continue to use the code to talk to each other.

Look in the yellow pages of the telephone book under the heading "Radio Communication Equipment and Systems." Sometimes electronic companies will sell telegraph keys. They will probably know the local amateur radio clubs in your area. You can write to the American Radio Relay League, 225 Main St., Newington, Connecticut 06111, for a free list of clubs near you or for free information about amateur radio. If you can't find a company that sells telegraph keys, then write directly to Radio Amateur Callbook, Inc., 925 Sherwood Drive, Lake Bluff, Illinois 60044.

Although Radio Shack doesn't sell telegraph sets, their Science Fair Project Kits include simple keys, while their Engineer's Mini-Notebook gives instructions on how to make a more complicated telegraph key. Radio Shack also sells small electronic buzzers. If you have trouble understanding the clickety-clack sounds of the Morse code using the telegraph set that you made following the instructions in this book, try making a set with a buzzer. Pick up a catalog at one of their stores or write to Radio Shack, 500 One Tandy Center, Fort Worth, Texas 76102.

Boy Scout troops too will have information on learning the Morse code, which is part of the requirements for the radio merit badge.

Finally, the Federal Communications Commission (FCC) is another source of information. The FCC has offices in large cities, and these offices issue amateur radio licenses.

FOR FURTHER READING

If you enjoyed learning about Samuel Morse, you might enjoy reading about radio, secret codes, and inventions.

Carter, Alden. *Radio: From Marconi to the Space Age.* New York: Watts, 1987.

Epstein, Sam. *The First Book of Electricity.* New York: Watts, 1977.

Garden, Nancy. *The Kid's Code and Cipher Book.* New York: Holt, 1981.

Janeczko, Paul B. *Loads of Codes and Secret Ciphers.* New York: Macmillan, 1984.

Macaulay, David. *The Way Things Work.* New York: Houghton Mifflin, 1988.

Mango, Karin. *Codes, Ciphers and Other Secrets.* New York: Watts, 1988.

Math, Irwin. *Morse, Marconi and You.* New York: Scribners, 1979.

Weiss, Harvey. *How to Be an Inventor.* New York: Crowell, 1980.

INDEX

59

ABOUT THE AUTHOR

Mona Kerby is an elementary school
teacher in Arlington, Texas.
She and her class had lots of fun
experimenting with the Morse code.